Maggie's Collection

This book is donated by

David Rochlin

in memory of
Maggie Adler
2007

Patterns in Nature

Day and Night

by Margaret Hall

Consulting Editor: Gail Saunders-Smith, PhD

Content Consultant: Dr. Ronald Browne, Associate Professor of Elementary Education
Minnesota State University, Mankato, Minnesota

Capstone

Mankato, Minnesota

Pebble Plus is published by Capstone Press,
151 Good Counsel Drive, P.O. Box 669, Mankato, Minnesota 56002.
www.capstonepress.com

Printed in the United States of America

1 2 3 4 5 6 11 10 09 08 07 06

Library of Congress Cataloging-in-Publication Data
Hall, Margaret, 1947–
Day and night / by Margaret Hall.
p. cm. —(Pebble plus. Patterns in nature)
Includes bibliographical references and index.
ISBN-13: 978-0-7368-6338-4 (hardcover)
ISBN-10: 0-7368-6338-9 (hardcover)
ISBN-13: 978-0-7368-9615-3 (softcover pbk.)
ISBN-10: 0-7368-9615-5 (softcover pbk.)
1. Earth—Rotation—Juvenile literature. 2. Day—Juvenile literature. 3. Night—Juvenile literature. 4. Pattern perception—Juvenile literature. I. Title. II. Series.
QB633.H35 2007
525'.35—dc22 2006001452

Summary: Simple text and photographs introduce how day and night occur and why they are one of nature's patterns.

Editorial Credits
Heather Adamson, editor; Kia Adams, designer; Renée Doyle, illustrator; Jo Miller, photo researcher; Scott Thoms, photo editor

Photo Credits
Corbis/Roger Ressmeyer, cover (moon); Roy Morsch, 14–15
Dwight R. Kuhn, 16–17
Getty Images Inc./The Image Bank/Romilly Lockyer, 18–19
PhotoEdit Inc./Myrleen Ferguson Cate, 13
Photos Researchers Inc./Adam Jones, 10–11
Shutterstock/Andrei Volkovets, 21 (day); Bobby Dailey, 21 (moon); Dmitry Brailovsky, cover (grass); Franzelin Fran-W., 21 (sunset); Keith Levit, 6–7; Nancy Tripp, 21 (sunrise); William Callis, 1; WizData Inc., backcover
SuperStock/age fotostock, 5

Note to Parents and Teachers

The Patterns in Nature set supports national science standards related to earth and life science. This book describes and illustrates day and night. The images support early readers in understanding the text. The repetition of words and phrases helps early readers learn new words. This book also introduces early readers to subject-specific vocabulary words, which are defined in the Glossary section. Early readers may need assistance to read some words and to use the Table of Contents, Glossary, Read More, Internet Sites, and Index sections of the book.

Table of Contents

Day or Night?

Look outside.

The sun lights the sky.

It is day.

But night is coming soon.

What makes day and night?

Earth spins, or rotates.
A full spin takes 24 hours,
or one whole day.
Day changes to night and
night to day as Earth spins.

Part of Earth faces the sun.
That part has day.
The other side faces away
from the sun.
It is night there.

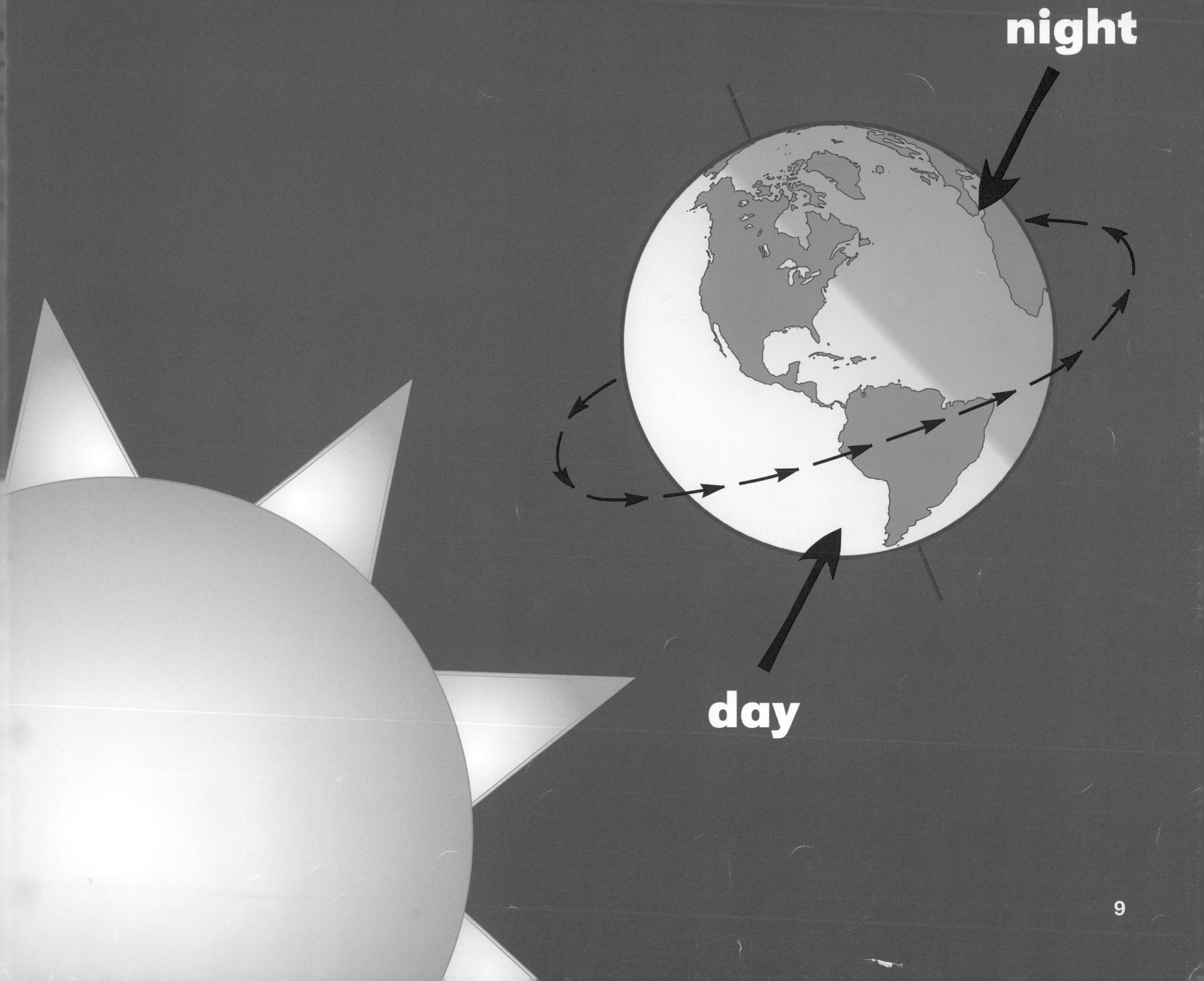

night

day

It's Day

The sun shines highest
in the sky at noon.
Sunshine warms Earth during
the day.
Sunlight helps plants grow.

Earth keeps spinning.
The part of Earth that had
day turns away from the sun.
The light fades in the sky
as the sun sets.

It's Night

Now the sky is dark.

The moon and stars glow.

People turn on lights

to help them see.

Night is longest in the winter.

Nocturnal animals

hunt at night.

Owls can see mice

in the dark.

Other animals sleep at night.

You sleep at night too.
Most people do.
When day comes again,
it's time to wake up.

It's a Pattern

Each day, the sun
rises and sets.
Night turning to day
is a pattern.
It happens again and again.

sunrise
day
sunset
night

Glossary

day—the time when your part of Earth faces the sun and the sky is light

Earth—the planet you live on

hunt—to look for food

night—the time when your part of Earth is turned away from the sun and the sky is dark

nocturnal—an animal that is active at night and rests during the day

pattern—something that happens again and again in the same order

rotate—to spin like a top; it takes 24 hours for Earth to spin completely around.

Read More

Bailey, Jacqui. *Sun Up, Sun Down: the Story of Day and Night.* Science Works. Minneapolis: Picture Window Books, 2004.

Kenah, Katherine. *Animals Day and Night.* Extreme Readers Series. Columbus, Ohio: McGraw-Hill Children's, 2004.

Internet Sites

FactHound offers a safe, fun way to find Internet sites related to this book. All of the sites on FactHound have been researched by our staff.

Here's how:

1. Visit *www.facthound.com*
2. Choose your grade level.
3. Type in this book ID **0736863389** for age-appropriate sites. You may also browse subjects by clicking on letters, or by clicking on pictures and words.

4. Click on the **Fetch It** button.

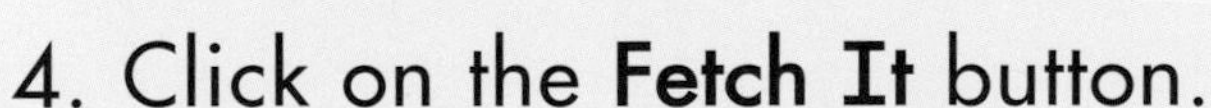

FactHound will fetch the best sites for you!

Index

Word Count: 188
Grade: 1
Early-Intervention Level: 15